D1356865

C333203563

Showdown in Moscow

– HUGH SHIELDS –

An environmentally friendly book printed and bound in England by
www.printondemand-worldwide.com

www.fast-print.net/store.php

Showdown in Moscow
Copyright © Hugh Shields 2012

ISBN 978-178035-328-9

First published 2012 by
FASTPRINT PUBLISHING
Peterborough, England.

Contents

Author's note

This book is not intended as a detailed, blow by blow account of the athletic careers of Seb Coe and Steve Ovett. Rather, it tries to capture the magic of their rivalry as it unfolded in the period up to the Moscow Olympics. For those readers looking for more detailed accounts, I would strongly recommend "The Perfect Race" by Pat Butcher and "Coe and Ovett File" by Mel Watman. I found both these books extremely useful as references and they provide fascinating insights into their respective careers. The only other books I have referred to while writing this are Ovett's autobiography and the book "Born to Run" by David Miller on Seb Coe.

This book is deliberately short and intended to be read in just a few hours. The account is concise so that, when you get the end, you have current recall of all their significant races and marvel at their achievements. To put it another way, the book is film-like in length and intended to register the same sort of effect as a film. So it is quite different in approach from the more detailed books mentioned above. Put simply, these few pages try to give the reader some Coe-Ovett magic in a book.

I have a number of people to thank. I would like to thank my family for accommodating the time I needed to write this. I would like to thank my parents for giving me a great start in life, including an excellent education. And I would like to thank Richard Bandler and his NLP colleagues – especially John and Kathleen La Valle – for giving me the additional impetus to complete this.

Hugh Shields

London, June 2012

Foreword

"It wasn't the Moscow Olympics. It was the Coe-Ovett Olympics." Dave Moorcroft, former 5000 metres world record holder.

This is the story of two of the world's greatest ever milers, Seb Coe and Steve Ovett. It culminates in their quest for gold at the 1980 Olympics in Moscow, by when they had firmly sealed their places in athletics history. For many, Coe and Ovett stand at the very pinnacle of all "supermilers". What makes the story so special is that they happened to be born within a year or so of each other in the same country.

Few who lived through the late 1970s and early 1980s in the UK can forget the media impact of Coe and Ovett. Many will remember watching their races with excitement, enlivened by the distinctive tones of commentators David Coleman and Ron Pickering. For their story was not chronicled in the low key pages of the tabloids or in recorded TV highlights at midnight. It was splashed across the front pages of the major British daily newspapers and commanded prime time television.

Before Moscow, Coe and Ovett had barely raced each other. They had, however, established impressive race credentials and traded world records. So when the Moscow Olympics came round, it was showdown time. It felt as if the entirety of the UK was on the edge of its seat – not to mention millions beyond these shores.

There is still no athletics clash which in living memory has come close to the Olympic duels of Coe and Ovett in Moscow.

Characterised in the press as the "good boy" (Coe) versus the "bad boy" (Ovett), their contrasting handling of the media made for excellent copy. Ovett would simply not speak to the press whereas for Coe, it was part of the deal. You made your own mind up, of course, as to whom you preferred. But make no mistake: most people had a view.

The combination of record-breaking runs and media hype generated huge public interest. And when, just weeks before the Olympics started, Ovett first broke and then equalled two of Coe's world records, the stage was set for the most titanic of Olympic duels.

The Coe-Ovett showdown in Moscow was, and still is, sporting theatre of the highest order.

The Making of Icons

Chapter One
3 Minutes 59.4 Seconds

"You've got something on your hands here boyo!"
UK coach Geoff Dyson to Ovett's coach Harry Wilson

By a strange quirk of fate, the first time Steve Ovett officially broke the 4 minute mile he was recorded at 3 minutes 59.4 seconds – exactly the same time Roger Bannister had run when breaking the barrier for the first time in history in 1954. The difference was that Ovett was only 18 years old compared to Bannister's more mature 26 years. In fact, it was possible that Ovett had already broken the barrier as a 17 year old when finishing just yards behind established UK international Nick Rose in a race at Motspur Park, the track made famous by the record-breaking Sydney Wooderson in the 1930s. Perhaps no one could quite believe that a 17 year old was capable of running that fast. So despite the fact that several onlookers had indeed recorded Ovett at 3 minutes 59 seconds, he was given an official time of 4 minutes 0.0 seconds. Ovett still became, at 18 a year later, the youngest Briton to have run a 4 minute mile.

From a young age, it was clear that Ovett had prodigious talent as a runner. Born in Brighton in 1955, he attended Varndean Grammar School and immediately began to make his mark as an athlete. The young Ovett took many English schools titles and put several UK age records to his name. He set a UK age 14 best of 1 minute 55 seconds in the 800 metres and subsequently ran 1 minute 52.5 seconds as a 16 year old. It was small wonder that UK coach Geoff Dyson later commented to Ovett's coach Harry Wilson: "You've got something on your hands here boyo!"

Ovett's talent had not gone unnoticed by a number of American universities, who were keen to sign him up for a sports scholarship. No fewer than 20 universities made offers. But Ovett, ever streetwise, immediately saw he would have to give something in return. Harry Wilson, who had by now begun his lifelong coaching relationship with Ovett, explained that the quid pro quo would be competing for the university two or three times a week during term times. Ovett cherished his independence and also realised that a "one size fits all" racing regime may well not be ideal for him. He rejected all 20 offers.

In 1973, aged 17, Ovett stepped up to his first major international championship, the European Junior Championships in Duisburg, Germany where he was due to run the 800 metres. Ovett had run some scintillating times by junior standards and he, along with most observers, regarded himself as favourite. Having cruised through the heats, he toed the line for the final expecting an untroubled victory. He settled into a good rhythm on the first lap and was well placed coming to the bell with one lap to go. But at this moment, two athletes came scorching past at a speed which took Ovett by surprise. These athletes were the Belgian Ivo Van Damme and the German Willy Wulbeck. Ivo Van Damme, who was tragically killed in a car accident in December 1976, won two silver medals in the 1976 Olympics while Willy Wulbeck would go on to become 800 metres gold medallist at the inaugural World

Athletics Championships in 1983. They were among the very finest.

Ovett dug in and focused on hunting them down. Ovett had sub-48 second 400 metres speed, which was exceptional for a junior middle distance runner, so it was going to take a lot to draw a sting from his tail. Slowly but surely, Ovett closed in on them and in the final 20 metres overhauled first Van Damme and then Willy Wulbeck on the line. The GB athletics coaches were ecstatic. Ovett had his first major win and so began a remarkable career of major international victories spanning over 15 years.

1974 and 1975 were both years of development for Ovett. He was getting faster and stronger all the time and had settled easily into senior competition. This was significant: many junior athletes found the transition to senior athletics extremely challenging. Some never make it, of course, and others can take years to make the transition effectively. But such was Ovett's talent that he slotted straight into the senior ranks without problem. Ovett had also begun to understand himself as an athlete. He knew what training worked for him and what did not. He had the ideal training partner in Matt Paterson and a shrewd sounding board in coach Harry Wilson. And he had the strong support of Andy Norman, the burly ex-policeman, who became the "Mr Fixit" of British athletics and could get Ovett into the right races at the right times. Ovett also used a potent mix of both high volume and high intensity training. The latter included punishing sessions on the sand dunes of Merthyr Mawr near Bridgend in Wales. Perhaps most importantly, Ovett could listen to his body and optimise his preparation in a way that other athletes are often unable to do. This robust foundation of training and self-awareness was what led Ovett to have one of the longest and most successful careers in middle distance athletics history. The highlight of this period was his silver medal in the 1974 European Championships in Rome and he had laid a solid base for the Olympics in 1976.

1976 was Olympic year in Montreal and Ovett had every intention of being there and doing well. The year did not start easily – Ovett was injured for three months – and he needed to bring all his talent to bear to be ready in time. But when it came to the trials at Crystal Palace in June, Ovett took victory in both the 800 metres and the 1500 metres. He had been left out of the team for the 1974 Commonwealth Games, apparently on account of his youth and inexperience. But this time, Ovett gave the selectors no option: he was indisputably an automatic choice for both events.

Ovett training on the sand dunes of Merthyr Mawr in Wales

Ovett with coach Harry Wilson

1974 European 800 metres championships

Ovett wins the 1976 Olympic 1500 metres trial

Arriving in Montreal, life in the Olympic village was a shock to the system for Ovett. There were three athletes to a room and life in the small apartment was claustrophobic. It was hardly ideal preparation. But it was the same for everyone and Ovett made the best of it.

The 800 metres in the Montreal Olympics was dominated by the giant Cuban athlete Alberto Juantorena. Juantorena was to run faster than Ovett ever would at this distance and was head and shoulders above the other athletes. There were other athletes who were quicker than Ovett as well. Nonetheless, Ovett came through the qualifying rounds unscathed and knew that, in the final, anything could happen.

Drawn in lane eight the odds were stacked against Ovett, for he would have to run most of the first lap "blind" and would be unable to judge the position of the other runners. Coming to the bell with one lap to go, Ovett was seventh and some way behind Juantorena. Ovett managed to pick off two runners to claim fifth. It had not been a vintage performance but on the other hand Juantorena had just set a new world record and Ovett could not realistically have done too much better.

The 1500 metres proved even more frustrating. In the semi-final, he tripped over another athlete who had fallen and was thus unable to qualify for the final. It was a sobering lesson in the harshness of the Olympics. But at least Ovett had other opportunities. He vowed things would be different next time.

The Montreal Olympics had been a formative experience for Ovett. He had worked through the unique pressure of the event and was more and more becoming the complete athlete. He knew he could take the world stage and make it his. But for how long and who would be his competition?

Ovett did not yet know that he would be joined by another highly talented British athlete. They had already raced each other in a schoolboy cross-country race in 1972 in which Ovett had come out on top. But this other athlete was a little younger, less mature for his age and biding his time. With his father Peter, Seb Coe was relentlessly transforming himself into a rival supermiler. It would not be long before Seb Coe became a big part of Ovett's running world.

Chapter Two
Not Without Ambition

"Thou art not without ambition but without the illness that should attend it." Lady Macbeth.

Frank Dick, one of the U.K.'s finest athletics coaches, frequently quotes Lady Macbeth when describing the supreme mental determination which separates champions from "also-rans". There is no doubt that Coe was born with this quality. It is the single ingredient that enabled him to overcome his darkest hours at the Moscow Olympics. It is the single ingredient that propelled him to 1500 metres gold for a second time at the Los Angeles Olympics. And it is the single ingredient that brought the Olympic Games to London in 2012.

If you ask an Olympic Champion why he or she has won gold, the athlete will nearly always talk about the mental aspects. No one ever talks about their physical capabilities, undoubted as these are among Olympic athletes. It is the pre-eminent contribution of the mind to Olympic success which is defining. To a great extent, the mind can be trained for success. But, to some people, the mind game comes naturally. It is part of their DNA and it marks them out for success even after great disappointment.

It is also sometimes said that you have to be lucky in your choice of parents. Coe no doubt inherited great qualities from both his parents. But the unique contribution of his father, Peter Coe, is essential to an understanding of the supermiler that Seb Coe became.

In 1970, when Coe was 14 and showing promise as a junior, Peter Coe mapped out a progressive series of times for the 1500 metres which he considered his son could achieve. These culminated in 3:30.0 in 1980, a time which was then several seconds faster than the world record. It is a time which is still indisputably world class today and very few have surpassed it. Seb Coe did indeed surpass it, although a little later than planned, when he ran 3:29.77 in 1986. It takes a unique personality to adopt such an approach. It takes an even more unique personality to accept it as read. Such was the power of this father-son relationship: these were two special talents combining into a force which would prove world-beating many times over.

Peter Coe was an engineer by training and profession. He had a methodical, even clinical, approach to his analysis of training methods. For him, if the evidence was there to support a particular approach, then he could accept it into his son's regime. But the hurdle the evidence had to clear was extremely high. Peter Coe also had one other advantage: he had no baggage as an athletics coach. And because he had no preconceived ideas of what was appropriate, he was prepared to open his mind to the very best training protocols, regardless of their source.

Peter Coe made no secret of his scientific methods and was open about the fact that he drew from various sources. For example he drew on the work of Dr John Humphreys to build an understanding of physiology and introduced blood analysis to monitor the effects of training on Seb. He also brought the study of biomechanics to bear and introduced a lot of conditioning work into Seb's regime. All of this, while quite standard now, was wholly unorthodox at the time and even frowned upon by some.

Seb put considerable emphasis on speed work and was an early and enthusiastic adopter of the so-called "five-pace" system of training developed by Frank Horwill, co-founder of the British Milers' Club. Under this system, the athlete does training sessions at speeds faster, slower and at actual race pace. The length of the training runs (or "intervals") varies to allow for the pace being run. Seb also did heavy weight training to improve his outright sprinting ability and generate more power from his wiry frame. Later in his career, he actually trained with sprinters at his club in Haringey in London. In fact, if you compare Seb Coe's training with that of Steve Ovett, a simplistic summary would be that the former emphasised speed and quality of training whereas Steve Ovett did a much higher volume of necessarily lower speed training. This is certainly one of the reasons why Seb Coe was a much superior 800 metres runner. Steve Ovett had phenomenal natural sprint speed and it is interesting to speculate whether, if he too had followed a path which put more emphasis on such speed, he would have been closer to Seb Coe at the shorter distance.

Coe competing at Loughborough University

Coe doing a 400 metres race

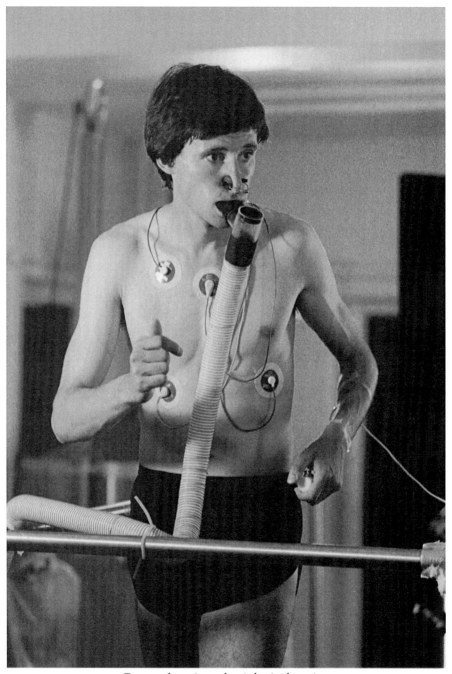

Coe undergoing physiological testing

Peter Coe

Peter Coe himself once commented that his unique contribution might have been to bring modern managerial skills to the coaching task. By this he meant setting detailed objectives and then putting detailed plans and resources into achieving them. Hard work and dedication - by both coach and athlete - were also critical ingredients. So it was that Seb trained remorselessly on the steep hills of Sheffield, even on Christmas day. He also trained with an intensity that was rare at the time, often running multiple repetitions with just a few seconds recovery in between.

There was one other vital ingredient which Peter Coe brought: a unique understanding of Seb. No other coach could have known Seb as well as Seb's own father and this understanding enabled Peter to fine-tune his son's training schedule in the most optimal way. In practice, this meant that Seb's training schedule was perfectly crafted to fit his racing schedule. The precise mix of training, the blending of discrete blocks (or periods) of training ("periodisation") and deft adjustments throughout were all the product of Peter's intimate understanding of his own son. No other coach could have done it.

The combination of talent and application brought immediate reward. As a 16 year old, in 1973, Coe won the English Schools' 3000 metres and also took a clutch of minor schoolboy titles. 1974 was a year of injury but Coe returned with a vengeance in 1975: he won the 1500 metres at the UK AAA Junior Championships and took bronze in the 1500 metres at the European Junior Championships later that year.

1976 was Olympic year and, aged 19, Coe had a shot at selection if he could build on his previous season. Unfortunately, it was not to be. By his own later standards, Coe ran an indifferent race in the 1500 metres and finished seventh in his heat, despite running a personal best time of 3 minutes 43.2 seconds. Nonetheless, the season as a whole continued to see him build and experiment. Coe was not afraid to lead from the front and, encouraged by his father, would frequently do so. It was only by doing this that he could truly find and expand his limits. So it was that, having set the early pace, he finished third in a mile race at Gateshead behind John Walker and Dave Moorcroft at Gateshead. Coe also led for three laps in the Emsley Carr Mile at Crystal Palace later that year. Although he faded to finish seventh in that race, he did have the satisfaction of beating 4 minutes for the first time with 3 minutes 58.3 seconds.

1977 was another year of building. Under university coach George Gandy, Coe was getting stronger through a judicious combination of weight training and speed work and was beginning to emerge as a major 800 metres runner. He started the year with some strong indoor performances, taking the AAA 800 metres title and winning some low-key international races. In March, Coe travelled to San Sebastian in Spain for the European Indoor Championships. After running comfortably in the heats, Coe led the final from the gun and took the gold medal in 1 minute 46.54 seconds. This was just a tenth of a second outside the indoor world record at the time and was Coe's first major international title. From now on all runners – not least Steve Ovett – would take Coe seriously.

In the outdoor summer season Coe ran consistently and well, showing glimpses of what was to come. He won the Emsley Carr Mile in 1977, running a personal best of 3 minutes 57.67 seconds and also becoming the youngest winner of the event. And at the end of the season, in the Coca Cola games at Crystal Palace, Coe clipped over a second from his personal best to take the UK 800 metres record for the first time in 1 minute 44.95 seconds. This record had previously belonged to Steve Ovett and, although Coe's 1500 metres times still lagged the best in the UK, this 800 metres performance marked the arrival of a serious talent.

By the end of 1977, then, Coe had laid the foundations for the supreme performances which were to come. His speed and strength work were beginning to pay off and, as he matured, he was simply getting faster naturally. Furthermore Coe was prepared to run fast from the front in order to discover his own limits, even if it meant he struggled towards the end of races. This experimentation with fast front running was another critical ingredient in the Coe story. His UK 800 metres record showed the approach was beginning to pay dividends. But how much faster could go Coe go? The world would not have to wait too much longer to find out.

Becoming Supermilers

Chapter Three

The Perfect Race

"Unbelievable, unbelievable! I've never seen acceleration like it."
Thomas Wessinghage, German 1500 metres record holder on
Ovett.

The highlight of the athletics year in 1977 was the World Cup which was scheduled to take place on September 3 in Düsseldorf. Ovett had performed strongly throughout the year, starting with a win in the Inter-Counties cross-country in January and continuing with some excellent track races throughout the summer. He also beat reigning Olympic 1500 metres champion and world record holder John Walker over 1 mile at the Debenham Games at Crystal Palace in London in June. This was a particularly popular win with the local British crowd: Ovett became the first Briton to beat John Walker at his preferred distance and also broke the UK mile record with a time of 3 minutes 54.7 seconds. It was a good day in the office.

Ovett's preparation also included a race which has gone down in athletics folklore and is testimony to the incredible versatility Ovett had as an all-round runner. On 20 August, just two weeks before the World Cup, Ovett had been due to race in Edinburgh. However, due to an airline strike, Ovett could not get there. Instead, he entered the Dartford Half Marathon with a last minute entry. It beggars belief that a middle distance athlete would compete in such a long race a mere fortnight before a major competition. But not only did Ovett compete, he won the race in 65 minutes and beat UK marathon champion Barry Watson in the process. As Coe later remarked, this episode fell nothing short of ripping the training manuals up in their entirety.

In order to run in the World Cup, Ovett had to be selected to represent Europe. Given his recent victories, including the European Cup Final 1500 metres in Helsinki in mid-August, one might have thought that selection would be a formality. However, this would be to assume away the ever-present politics of selection - selectors did not always do what logic might suggest. On this occasion, there was some strong lobbying from the Eastern Europeans for the selection of Josef Plachy of Czechoslovakia. Plachy was a fine athlete but very few dispassionate observers would put him above Ovett. After some jockeying for position - and an ultimatum from GB coach Dennis Watts that he would resign if Ovett was not selected – Ovett got the nod from the selectors.

Apart from Ovett, the main protagonists in the World Cup race were John Walker and Thomas Wessinghage. John Walker, the charismatic "flying Kiwi", was the world mile record holder and Olympic champion over 1500 metres. He was the first man to break 3 min 50 seconds and was a prolific racer over the distance. In total he broke the four-minute barrier well over 100 times. Ovett had already defeated Walker earlier in the season and thus Walker would be all out to avenge that defeat.

The other protagonist was the German Thomas Wessinghage. In another era, Wessinghage would have picked up many more gold medals. However Coe and Ovett's dominance denied him.

In 1980 he set a German record of 3:31.58 minutes for 1500 metres which to this day remains a German national record.

Wessinghage and Walker knew that to defeat Ovett, they would have to go out hard from the start in an effort to draw the sting from Ovett's trademark kick. By 1977, Ovett's finishing kick - administered somewhere around the 200 metres mark - had become absolutely lethal. Able to cover the penultimate 100 metres of the race in under 12 seconds, Ovett had found the ability to take 20 metres out of his opponents in that short distance. This electrifying acceleration was humbling to his opponents, who realised they could never match it no matter how hard they trained. It was a depressing realisation for those in pursuit of the very top.

Wessinghage and Walker recognised the problem and decided to collaborate. It is virtually unheard of for athletes from different countries and teams to do this. But it reflected Ovett's dominance at the time and both Wessinghage and Walker felt good about it. It would give them a chance of victory in a race in which their defeat was all but assured. Together they agreed they would set off at their fastest possible tempo, around 56 seconds per lap.

The conditions for the race were perfect. It was a windless and warm evening and the largely German crowd were looking for a great performance from their very own local athlete. It would need to be a great performance from Wessinghage for he was up against two of the all-time greats.

As planned, Wessinghage set off fast on the first lap. John Walker then took the lead up to 1000 metres, at which point another athlete, Dave Hill, took up the running. At the bell, the 1100 metres mark, Ovett moved into third position just behind Walker. Wessinghage was still running well in fourth. With 200 metres to go, sensing Walker was about to make a move, Ovett turned on the afterburners. This was another level of running power altogether. He left the field trailing instantly and helplessly in his wake. You had to see it to believe it and, even when you did, it took your breath away. With 80 metres to go, Ovett had surprised even himself to discover that he had a 20 metre lead and he continued down the home straight to cross the line in 3 min 34.5 seconds. It was a UK record and just two seconds outside the world record.

The world will never know what time Ovett would have run that night if he had run at his maximum even tempo right from the start. But Ovett himself said that the race felt easy throughout and he didn't even push it all the way to the line: in what had become something of an Ovett trademark, he had waved casually to the crowd some 40 metres out.

For the other athletes this was also a watershed moment. John Walker had simply stepped off the track when Ovett pressed the accelerator, apparently overwhelmed by the speed of Ovett's finish. And Wessinghage generously went over to Ovett at the end of the race to tell him: "Unbelievable, unbelievable! I've never seen acceleration like it." Ovett knew that on that summer's night no one in the world could have beaten him.

As Ovett came off the track he was greeted by Dennis Watts, who had been reduced to tears by this supreme performance. Geoff Dyson, who at one point had been Britain's chief national coach, opined that this race should be shown as the definitive example of middle-distance running. Ovett truly had arrived. If anyone was to challenge this level of performance, they would have to demonstrate running powers which had never been seen before. Remarkably, just two years later, this is exactly what happened.

Chapter Four
41 Days of Magic

"The way he ran was just unbelievable. He looked like he could run under 1:40. He never tied up at all." John Walker, Olympic 1500 metres champion and world record holder, on Coe.

On 5 July 1979, Seb Coe electrified the world of athletics. On a perfect summer's evening in the famous Bislet Stadium in Oslo, Coe ran 1 minute 42.33 seconds for 800 metres, decimating the existing record set by Alberto Juantorena by over a second. Athletics fans around the world stood up and took notice. A very special talent had just arrived.

Coe's world record was somewhat unheralded. In the previous year, he had finished third in the European Cup 800 metres race, losing out to both Ovett and the East German Olaf Beyer. Coe had given a small hint of what was to come in that race, covering the first lap in a very fast 50 seconds before "blowing up" on the second lap. The difference in 1979 was that Coe was able to keep the pace going right through to the finishing line. Beyer surprised both the British athletes that day and afterwards Ovett had gone over to Coe, appearing to commiserate. In fact, as Ovett revealed many years later in a breakfast conversation with Seb during the Melbourne Commonwealth Games of 2006, he had said: "Who the **** was that?!" Ovett made up later in those championships by taking gold in the 1500 metres, a race in which Coe did not compete. The 800 metres race was to be their only track race before the Moscow Olympics, a fact which only served to increase interest in their "virtual" rivalry.

You could not really call Coe's record-breaking Oslo run a "race". It was a procession. Coe set off at a scarcely believable pace, covering the first lap in 50.6 seconds and tearing the field apart as he did so. The other competitors may perhaps have reasoned that Coe would fade, as he had in the European Cup race the year before. But this time he kept the relentless pace going and by the time he reached the finish line was well over 30 metres clear of the entire field. The sense of collective excitement in the crowd was palpable. They had just witnessed one of the truly great performances in middle-distance running history.

What made the record remarkable was the fact that it was still relatively early season for Coe and he had only just finished his final degree exams. Coe himself considered he was only about 80% fit – a fact he had confided before the race to Chris Brasher of 4 minute mile pacing fame – and in some recent weeks had gone down to just two days a week training. In normal circumstances, this was not the kind of build-up that resulted in records. For those who knew even a little bit about middle-distance running, the question was obvious: where could this possibly lead?

Coe breaks the 800 metres world record in Oslo, July 1979

Coe breaks the mile world record in Oslo, July 1979

Coe after one of his many victories

Coe breaks the 1500 metres world record in Zurich, August 1979

The Oslo run was a vindication of Peter Coe's philosophy of constantly pushing Seb's boundaries. It is partly a physical thing. We know that the human body can adapt incrementally to greater physical efforts over time. But it is also a mental thing. If you can truly open yourself up to the possibility of superior performance then, when those superior performances start to come, the mind grows accustomed to the success and welcomes more.

The immediate question of where this would lead was soon to be answered. On 17 July, Coe returned to the Bislet Stadium to run the high-profile "dream mile". The field contained most of the world's great milers at that time, although Steve Ovett was notable by his absence and claimed the race would be hollow without him. The American Steve Scott, the New Zealander John Walker and the German Thomas Wessinghage were all there, along with a number of other leading US and European athletes.

The athletics world was fascinated by this race: Coe was a specialist 800 metres runner and was clearly moving into unknown territory. He had raced only four times over this distance in the previous four seasons. Given his background, it was generally felt he would get to the halfway point very fast but would fade on the third lap.

Peter Coe instructed Seb to get near the front, see what happened and aim to win. They were not particularly focused on another world record. As the gun went, the field was led off by the American Lacy. The pace was fast but controlled and by the end of the second lap, Coe was lying in fourth with most of the field still very much in contention. At this point, Steve Scott put in an injection of pace and broke the field – or at least, most of it. Coe was following Scott, seemingly in control and looking effortless and relaxed. Scott and Coe covered the third lap in around 58 seconds. As they reached the bell, Coe moved easily past Scott and it was now clear that if he could complete the last lap in 56 seconds, a second world record would be his.

Coe was by now pouring the pace on and the specialist milers could do nothing but hang on as best they could. Coe raced down the final straight to cross the line in 3 min 48.95 seconds, just inside John Walker's record of 1975. Coe had taken his second world record inside a fortnight and left the world's best milers trailing in his wake.

Coe's second record came as a surprise to some. Many observers had not expected Coe to be able to go the distance. Even for Seb and Peter Coe, it was clearly a breakthrough performance and marked a decisive moment in his quest for Olympic glory. But Peter Coe had been planning this kind of performance for years. It was not so much a surprise as a natural progression in his eyes.

Having obliterated the 800 metres world record, and taken the mile record from John Walker, it was obvious that Coe would seek the 1500 metres record as well to cap his season in style. Along with Oslo and Brussels, Zurich is the other city in which middle distance records have frequently been set. Zurich's Weltklasse meeting has a rich history and was one of the first large international meetings to take place outside the Olympics. Sometimes referred to as the "one day Olympics", the Weltklasse was first held in 1928 and routinely attracts the world's best athletes. For all these reasons, it was an obvious place for Coe to head on 15 August 1979.

As a double world record holder, Coe faced a new issue for the first time: he was expected to break the world record and the crowd would go away disappointed if he did not. When the gun sounded, Coe immediately set off at a fast, even tempo and enjoyed the vocal support of the knowledgeable Zurich crowd. Coe did not let up this pace and reached the bell on schedule. By now, the noise of the crowd had become deafening. Urged on by his father, Coe dug deep on the final lap. But he showed little sign of strain and, as he came down the home straight, maintained perfect form. Coe crossed the finishing line just a fraction of a second inside the previous world record, stopping the clock at 3 minutes 32.1.

In a magical purple patch of 41 days Coe had taken three world records, a feat no other athlete had previously achieved at these distances. At the start of the season, Coe had been relatively well-known to serious athletics fans. By the end of this incredible period, Coe had become a world superstar. How would Steve Ovett respond? The athletics world was fascinated to find out.

Chapter Five
The Guns Are Loaded

"Serious sport is war minus the shooting."

George Orwell.

Compared to Coe's dazzling season, the year 1979 was inevitably less high profile for Ovett. Nonetheless, he won the famous Emsley Carr Mile, broke the UK record for 1000 metres and ran some very fast mile and 1500 metres races. In particular, at the Ivo Van Damme memorial meeting in Brussels on September 4, Ovett came tantalisingly close to Coe's 1500 metres world record when he finished just eight hundredths of a second outside it. That race, especially, was a significant morale booster in a season where the headlines had been dominated by Coe. It was a good platform year ahead of the Olympics in 1980.

On July 1 1980, just three weeks before the Olympics, both Coe and Ovett went out to the Bislet Stadium in Oslo. However, in a portent of their careful avoidance of each other in years to come, they were not entered in the same race. Coe had decided to do the 1000 metres while Ovett was entered for the mile. Coe's race came first. He immediately brought the crowd alight with another dazzling display and another world record. Coe now had four world records to his name. The crowd's anticipation for the mile was suitably piqued.

Ovett had always said that he preferred to run against people rather than against the clock. However Coe's achievements in 1979 meant that Ovett could no longer ignore times. Ovett set out deliberately to break the world mile record in Oslo that evening. In a sense, he needed to do so in order to strike a psychological blow ahead of the Olympics. Dave Warren from the UK was to act as pacemaker. In addition, there were two other Britons in the race in the form of Steve Cram and Graham Williamson, for whom this was a personal Olympic trial to determine who would join Coe and Ovett in Moscow. Ovett immediately set off at a very fast pace and went through the halfway point in 1 minute 52.8 seconds, a shade faster than Coe had run in his world record run the previous year. Ovett now had to run the last two laps on his own and, with the encouragement of the delirious crowd, kept the relentless pace going while looking relaxed and comfortable. That night, Ovett was running in the "zone", that trance-like state where everything feels easy and the world can be blocked out. Ovett finally crossed the line in 3 minutes 48.8 seconds to take Coe's record and the rapturous applause of the crowd. Coe had held four records for barely an hour.

Ovett breaks the mile world record in July 1980

Ovett in full flight

Ovett wins the Bannister mile in May 1980

Ovett training at one of his favoured locations

Two weeks later, on 15 July, Ovett returned to the same stadium. He had been feeling good in training and felt that he could take the 1500 metres record as well, thereby striking a decisive blow ahead of the games. Ovett followed the early pace and they went through three laps about a second outside Coe's world record pace. But it was the last lap that made the difference. Ovett scorched round in 56.1 seconds which, given his wave to the crowd on the home straight, was seriously fast. The time Ovett ran that night could not have been scripted better by Hollywood. Ovett precisely equalled Coe's world record, running 3 minutes 32.1 seconds and throwing another gauntlet down to Coe. With just days before the Olympics started in Moscow, the guns were now well and truly loaded for one of the most fascinating showdowns in Olympic history.

Moscow

Chapter Six
The Art of the Impossible

"The most naturally talented athlete I ever raced against, by a distance." Coe's view of Ovett.

Hugh Shields

Ovett woke up in the Olympic village to find another hot day in Moscow. Everything had gone smoothly in getting this far. The only potential problem had been the possibility of a government-mandated boycott of the games in protest at the Soviet invasion of Afghanistan. But this had been averted, largely due to some vocal lobbying from the athletes themselves. The government decided to leave participation at the discretion of the athletes and, in the end, most decided to go.

Ovett's form could not be better and his training had gone well. You only had to look at his recent races to see that the showdown with Coe was going to be something special. Importantly, too, he was mentally well-adjusted for the first big clash. Ovett wanted gold in the 800 metres. And he was going to go all out to get it. True, his personal best was around 1.5 seconds slower than Coe - a significant amount at this rarefied level of competition. Many athletes would have written off their chances before even lining up for the race. But Ovett was no ordinary athlete. He never turned up to be an "also-ran". He raced to win. And this could be the biggest win of the lot.

After taking his morning run and breakfast, Ovett took a wander around the village with coach Harry Wilson. It was primarily a waiting game now. Ovett also had the media gauntlet to run - press interest was intense. He donned a pair of dark glasses and kept his profile low. There was not too much Wilson could do at this point other than offer positive messages of reinforcement.

Perhaps Ovett's previous Olympic experience would prove invaluable in Moscow. In any event, his preparation had been flawless. Moscow was all about execution - delivering the races as planned. His positive mind set at this point meant that it would take a Herculean effort from Coe to stop him.

Ovett was used to running twice a day and he continued this regime religiously. His actual fitness levels would not change now - the body needs 10 to 14 days for the effects of training to translate into improved fitness. Ovett was, in any case, in the peak of condition. What mattered now was routine, relaxation and focus on the matter in hand. Meanwhile, the press was desperate to get Ovett to do an interview. It would make quite an exclusive because it was Ovett's habit not to talk to the press at all. To Ovett, the media was an intrusion and could usually add nothing to his race preparation. He could hardly care less. His exchanges in recent years had been limited and sometimes derisory. In 1977, after the World Cup, he was asked if he would like to convey any message to the press. The answer came back: "Happy Christmas!" Despite this history with the press Ovett decided that, in the unique pressure cooker of the Olympics, a well-placed interview might give an edge. Ovett decided to speak to the BBC and took the opportunity to tell the world how relaxed and confident he was. This is exactly the kind of talk which would strike fear into his rivals, Coe included. Everyone could see that Ovett was supremely fit in a physical sense. Now they could see he was supremely strong in a mental sense as well. Who could bet against him?

The expectations on Coe in the 800 metres were immense. He was the world record holder and had decimated every field he had come up against since September 1978 when he had broken the UK record at Crystal Palace. Coe was not just a little bit faster than everyone else in Moscow - he was over two seconds faster. That translates to some 15 metres at Coe's top 800 metres pace. This race ought to be a formality for Coe. He just had to get out there and do it.

Peter Coe had been plotting this Olympic moment since Coe was 14. This was the culmination of a decade of carefully planned training, a fact which was itself adding to the pressure of the games. This race was Coe's to lose. When it came to the press Coe made himself freely available, although even he was a little surprised when 500 journalists turned up for one meeting. Coe was used to giving press interviews - he was the "good guy" compared to "bad guy" Ovett depicted by the press. "How easily will you win the 800 metres?" "Do you think you will beat your world record?" "Are you worried about Ovett?" The questions kept coming and Coe kept answering. But could this really be regarded as helpful preparation? One thing is certain: it did not help him relax. On the contrary, this type of questioning made the nerves go into overdrive. Coe needed to relax and focus ahead of the big challenge. Instead he found his nerves running wild.

Both Coe and Ovett qualified comfortably for the final. That was the easy part. On the day of the final itself, the British newspapers were brimming with Coe-Ovett coverage. This was the moment it seemed the whole country - indeed the entire athletics world - had been waiting for. Unsurprisingly, the papers took different views of the outcome. For some, Coe's superior 800 metres speed would prove decisive. For others, Ovett's unparalleled racing ability and killer instinct would make the difference. Whichever athlete you supported, the anticipation and excitement surrounding this race was simply immense. People watch sport because of the possibility of a titanic contest which keeps you on the edge of your seat. This was just such a sporting contest – two world record holders, each with phenomenal racing achievements, going head to head. Even better, they came from the same country and displayed apparently different characters. It was small wonder that press interest was running so high.

Ovett keeps a low profile at the Moscow Olympics

Ovett takes the Olympic 800 metres title

Ovett savours his 800 metres victory

The 800 metres medal ceremony

Coe paced around nervously with his father after breakfast at the Olympic Village. The occasion was definitely getting to him. It is not easy being the overwhelming favourite. And when the occasion happens to be your first ever Olympic final, the nerves are going to be fragile. Coe's problem was that his nerves had been fragile for several days now. It wasn't pleasant and he just wanted the race over and done with.

The athletes gathered in the call-up area underneath the Central Lenin Stadium. It is a difficult time for athletes. The adrenalin is flowing and, typically, the athlete prefers to jog around and continue warming up. But in the confines of the call-up area, this is rarely possible. Instead athletes must stay in the designated area biding their time and trying to remain focused. Races can be won or lost at this point: the mental game is everything at Olympic level. The gold medallist remains totally focused, undistracted by what is going on around him and filled with positive thoughts and imagery. By contrast the "also-rans" may be allowing negative thoughts to creep in and are already entertaining the possibility of defeat. Staying in the gold medal zone requires supreme mental strength at this level of competition. Very few can do it and on that day it looked like Ovett, who had nonchalantly turned up 10 minutes after the others, was there. With Coe, it was not at all clear. Ovett believed he would win, whereas Coe worried he might lose.

The 800 metres final was not a two horse race - no Olympic athletics final ever really is. There was another British athlete, Dave Warren. He had done well to make the final and would give 110%. The home crowd had Nikolay Kirov to support. He wanted to give the locals something to cheer about and beating Coe and Ovett would surely do that - not to mention the huge political symbolism and kudos which would go with it. There were four other athletes in the race. If either Coe or Ovett had a bad day at the office, any of these other athletes could steal gold. But they would have to steal it because either Coe or Ovett was the rightful owner. The full line-up, in the order of their semi-final qualifying times, was as follows:

Steve Ovett (GBR) 1:46.6

Nikolay Kirov (URS) 1:46.6

Sebastian Coe (GBR) 1:46.7

Detlef Wagenknecht (GDR) 1:46.7

Andreas Busse (GDR) 1:46.9

Agberto Guimarães (BRA) 1:46.9

Dave Warren (GBR) 1:47.2

José Marajo (FRA) 1:47.3

Having been checked off, the eight athletes were led out into the main arena of the Central Lenin Stadium. You could sense the excitement in the crowd: this was a defining moment in the Moscow Olympics. Back in the UK and elsewhere millions clustered around TV sets with exactly the same thought. Millions also registered two other things: Ovett looked cool and calm whereas Coe was anything but. The confidence was simply radiating from Ovett whereas Coe looked as if he would rather not be there. Millions saw these things although not so many read them. But already it was clear: Ovett had the look of a winner.

Mental rehearsal is a big part of the winning sports performance. You picture yourself running the perfect race and the race itself becomes an exercise in execution. On this day, Ovett had nailed it before the race had even begun. He had the reputation of being the supreme racer and, notwithstanding his killer finishing speed, his mental toughness was the reason why. Of course, it is a little easier to be mentally tough when you are blessed with God-given physical talent and have honed it to perfection. But the mental piece is still the critical part of the jigsaw and no amount of physical superiority can replace it.

The athletes were ready to go and a heady mix of anticipation and tension gripped the crowd. Part one of the Coe-Ovett Moscow story was about to unfold. All eight athletes leaned forward in their individual lanes, the fronts of their running spikes pushed right up to the start line so as not to lose even an inch of possibility. They were on their marks, then set to go. Pulses were racing among athletes and spectators alike. Then came the gun and the athletes were off on their journey into athletics history.

The athletes rounded the first bend and, down the back straight, came out of their lanes and settled into the race. Ovett positioned himself near the front as Dave Warren, the third British athlete, led the field round the first lap. Worryingly Coe was right at the back of the field, apparently trying to stay out of trouble. At the bell, with one lap to go, Coe was still at the back and did not seem engaged. He would have to do something quickly because, when the first move came, he would be too far back to respond. Kirov was now leading and the local crowd were warming seriously to the potential for Soviet victory. As they moved into the back straight Ovett - still well-positioned - got boxed in by one of the other athletes. He, too, would have to do something quickly - and he did. With an elbow here and a shoulder there, he forced himself between the athletes boxing him in and got right onto the shoulder of Kirov.

Seconds later, Kirov made his run for home. The local crowd were delirious. But they must surely have known that a Kirov victory was an impossibility. He was being tracked by the supreme racer of all and Ovett, with his lethal finishing kick, would be unstoppable in a few moments. As they rounded the final bend, Coe suddenly came into the picture for the first time. Coming from the back of the field with 200 metres to go, Coe came scorching through the field at phenomenal speed, the mental pain etched on his face. But surely there was too much ground to make up, extraordinary 800 metres runner though he was. With about 80 metres to go, Ovett struck. He hit the front and, with every ounce of commitment, raced for the line. Coe was gaining but the gap was too much and Kirov was now clear in third. Ovett crossed the line and took what appeared to be the simplest of victories. He had achieved the art of the impossible: beating Coe over 800 metres.

.

Chapter Seven
Trail of Shame

"Mind is everything: muscle – pieces of rubber. All that I am, I am because of my mind." Paavo Nurmi, multiple Olympic gold medallist.

By the time of the medal ceremony Coe was, understandably, completely disconsolate. Having been beaten in his favoured event, it was all he could do to muster a handshake with Ovett. By his own assessment, Coe had run the worst race of his life.

It is virtually unheard of in athletics to recover from this kind of defeat in a matter of days. Normally, a period of reflection and rebuilding is required. So if Coe was going to strike gold in the 1500 metres, he would have to climb a mountain to do so. And the climb would have to take place under the fiercest of public spotlights. Coe had become famous for his physical prowess. But this challenge was different. It was entirely of the mind.

Immediately after the race, Peter Coe vented considerable frustration. Some of this was directed at himself. How could he have failed to prepare Seb properly for the 800 metres? What more could he have done? And more importantly, what was he now to do to get Seb ready for the 1500 metres? Peter remained convinced of one thing: Seb still had all the weapons. In this respect, nothing had changed. But could Seb draw on these weapons? Somehow, together, they had to find a way.

There were a few days before the qualifying rounds of the 1500 metres and Peter decided that hard training was the best course of action. They would literally run the 800 metres defeat out of Seb's system.

The day after the final Daley Thompson, who won gold in the decathlon at Moscow, paid Coe an unannounced visit. Going over to the window, he opened the curtains. Coe asked: "What's the weather like?" Thompson replied: "Oh, it all looks a bit silver to me!" This was exactly the reality check Coe needed. Nobody had died. It was only a race. By putting the 800 metres result in perspective, Coe could re-build.

Soon afterwards, Coe went off for a 10 mile run and began the re-building process. He was trailed for a considerable part of the way by a posse of photographers in a car. The next day, one of the British tabloids ran the headline: "Coe's Trail of Shame".

As the qualifying rounds of the 1500 metres neared, Coe turned a corner. He decided to deliver his very best performances in the coming days. He knew that if he could do that, he at least would be able to live with himself. He had not worked this hard for 10 years simply to throw in the towel. The alternative - giving in to the mental battle - had all kinds of downsides which would cast a long dark shadow over his future. This could not be countenanced. Instead, he promised himself he would never leave a track feeling as disappointed with his performance as he was with the 800 metres final. It was a personal commitment of the greatest conviction. He also reasoned that, statistically, the chances that he would run a second race as poorly as the 800 metres final were slim.

The British press, meanwhile, continued its frenetic interest in the Coe-Ovett saga. By now, few gave Coe a chance in the longer distance. It seemed almost inevitable that Ovett would triumph again - the 1500 metres was, after all, the event he had dominated for three years now.

With Coe now back in the right mental zone and Ovett seemingly as strong as ever, the stage was set for the enthralling rematch. The public could barely wait.

Chapter Eight
Redemption

"Without question the greatest middle-distance runner we have had in the UK." Ovett's view of Coe.

On the morning of the final, the British newspapers were buzzing with comment and anticipation. Most concluded that Ovett would do the double. How could it be otherwise? The evidence was compelling. Ovett had just beaten Coe in the latter's specialist event and, furthermore, had not been beaten over 1500 meters for 3 years now - a sequence of 45 races in total. It was also now clear that Ovett's ability to handle the pressure of the Olympics was simply greater than Coe's. To cap it all, many felt that Ovett's tactical brain and racing instincts were superior. All these factors combined to make Ovett the overwhelming favourite.

Ovett himself had continued to exude confidence in the qualifying heats. He looked relaxed and completely dominant every time he set foot on the track. He moved relaxed and effortlessly through the early rounds, always looking controlled and running well within his limits. His mastery of tactical positioning in the 1500 metres race was undoubted. He knew when to lay off the pace, how to re-position himself when boxed in and what was necessary to take total control of the race towards the finish. He also had every weapon in the armoury. He could run at a sustained fast pace - that is why he had equalled the world record earlier that year. But, off a slower race, he could also put in an electrifying burst of speed from 200 metres out. He did all of this while looking totally at ease and, as if to add insult to injury, he would send an "I love you" signal to his girlfriend, Rachel, at the end of each heat. The message was clear: I am having fun, I am confident, I am unbeatable.

Coe was also qualifying easily in the early rounds. Even under duress in the 800 metres final he was impressive to watch. Powerful and biomechanically perfect, Coe glided around the track looking every inch the multiple world record holder that he was. But could he marry his undoubted physical ability with the mental strength that would be needed to win gold? Most people doubted it for the simple reason that they had seen evidence to the contrary in the 800 metres final. If Coe could not be mentally strong in the 800 metres, where his best times were completely dominant, how could he expect to be strong in the 1500 metres where Ovett was just as fast?

In the semi-finals, Coe and Ovett qualified for the final comfortably enough. On this occasion, Ovett actually had to work a bit to maintain his unbeaten record – might he perhaps have had to work just a little bit too hard to make the final? The athletics world was about to find out.

When Coe and Ovett left the Olympic village for the stadium, press interest was at fever pitch. British and foreign journalists alike were riveted, hanging on their every move. This was pressure of untold proportions.

Coe and Ovett were not the only Britons in the race for Steve Cram had also qualified for the final. Aged only 19, Cram had produced a remarkable effort to get there. Cram had worked hard just to make the Olympic squad: Graham Williamson, another supremely talented teenager, had almost beaten Cram to it but had lost out in the Oslo race earlier in July. Now Cram was set to play his role in one of the great moments of modern Olympic history.

The competitors in the final, in the order of their semi-final qualifying times, were as follows:

1. Sebastian Coe (GBR) 3:39.4

2. Jürgen Straub (GDR) 3:39.4

3. José Marajo (FRA) 3:39.6

4. Vittorio Fontanella (ITA) 3:40.1

5. Jozef Plachý (TCH) 3:40.4

6. Steve Ovett (GBR) 3:43.1

7. Dragan Zdravkovi? (YUG) 3:43.4

8. Andreas Busse (GDR) 3:43.5

9. Steve Cram (GBR) 3:43.6

The Olympic 1500 metres final

Straub bids for victory in the 1500 metres final

Coe takes the Olympic 1500 metres title

The 1500 metres medal ceremony

The athletes warmed up and readied themselves for one last supreme effort. Neither Coe nor Ovett was giving too much away. But there was no question that the body language was different, especially from Coe. Could he really have found the strength not only to recover from defeat but also to visualise victory in his less favoured event? And was Ovett in the same frame of mind as the 800 metres? He chatted almost nervously in the call-up zone, telling Coe that they must go for a drink after it was all over. Coe, locked in a world of focus and concentration, barely answered.

With the crowd hushed in anticipation and millions glued to the television at home, the gun sounded. Straub immediately went to the front and was followed by Coe. Although running in procession, the pace was relatively sedate by the standards of these athletes. As they came into the home straight for the first time, Straub and Coe still led the field. Marajo and Ovett followed with Cram and the other athletes just behind.

The second lap continued at this steady pace with very little change in order. Cram ran at Ovett's shoulder but there was no break just yet. A waiting game continued and the crowd watched enthralled. At some point, the big move was going to come and, when it did, most of the athletes would be found wanting. The beauty of 1500 metres racing is that the variety of potential tactics is vast. This combination of unpredictability and uncertainty makes the event fascinating.

Straub passed 800 metres in just under 2 min 5 seconds. At that very moment, he picked up the pace and incrementally accelerated over the next lap in a bid to drop Coe and Ovett. It was a bold move, especially when you have the two fastest athletes in the world right behind you. But the race was on and Straub meant business. Covering the third lap in a little over 54 seconds, the field had been strung ruthlessly apart. Could anyone other than Coe and Ovett live with this pace?

Coe followed Straub at this relentless place with Ovett in third. The endless fascination of this great duel continued as they scorched down the back straight to the deafening noise of the crowd. Straub was making another push for home and perhaps - just perhaps - the pace was beginning to tell in favour of Coe.

With 150 metres to go, Coe unleashed a ferocious burst of speed which took him simultaneously clear of both Straub and Ovett. Coe was now flying and, coming off the bend, kicked again. Ovett was still in third and seemingly unable to make up ground on either Coe or Straub. Coe now needed to maintain his form to take victory. If there was one athlete who could be relied on to do this at such speed, it was Coe. Within moments, Coe crossed the line to take what many had believed to be an impossible gold medal.

Coe dropped to his knees in relief more than fatigue. A huge burden had been lifted from his shoulders and his place in athletics history was assured. Had Coe been beaten that day by Ovett, it is possible his reputation would never have recovered. But Coe had now proved, to himself as much as anything, that his phenomenal physical prowess was matched by remarkable inner mental strength. This rare combination would take Coe on to still greater heights in future years. The world had just witnessed the arrival of middle-distance greatness.

Ovett smiled wryly and acknowledged Coe's victory in generous spirit. Since his victory in the 800 metres he had lost some of his mental focus and, in the heat of Olympic competition, that will always be telling. But Ovett could put defeat in perspective and was returning to Britain with an Olympic gold medal. Life was not exactly bad.

The world had been privileged to see this remarkable athletics rivalry in full blossom. As they took their respective medals on the rostrum, few could know that the competition between them would never manifest itself again in quite such dramatic circumstances. Their rivalry certainly did continue and, in 1981, they famously traded the world mile record three times in ten days. But it was in Moscow that they spun their most enthralling and entertaining magic.

Postscript: Forever Fast

.

Today, over 25 years after they ran their fastest times, Coe and Ovett's personal bests still rank with the top runners in the world. It is remarkable that, were they competing now, they would still be at the very top of their events. Outside the 800 and 1500 metres, there is no other distance in men's athletics in which this can be said.

For the record their best times over 1500 metres, run several years after the Moscow Olympics, would have topped the 2011 world rankings:

3:29.77 Seb Coe Rieti 7 Sep 1986

3:30.77 Steve Ovett Rieti 4 Sep 1983

3:31.86 Haron Keitany Hengelo 29 May 2011

3:31.90 Mekonnen Gebremedhin Hengelo 29 May 2011

3:31.92 Amine Laalou Torino 10 Jun 2011

In the 800 metres, where Coe's superior speed compared to Ovett is clear, Coe would have ranked second only to David Rudisha in 2011:

1:41.33 David Rudisha Rieti 10 Sep 2011

1:41.73 Seb Coe Florence 10 Jun 1981

1:43.13 Abubaker Kaki London 05 Aug 2011

1:43.15 Asbel Kiprop Monaco 22 Jul 2011

In the 800 metres, only two athletes – David Rudisha and Wilson Kipketer – have ever run faster than Coe, which is a considerable tribute to the quality of his performances at the shorter distance. Ovett, with a best 800 metres time of 1:44.09, would have ranked 12th in the world in 2011. Of course, were they actually running today, they would be benefiting from all the advances in training and equipment that have occurred over the years. It is fascinating to speculate just how fast they would be.

People often ask which athlete was superior. The majority give the verdict to Coe on account of his greater number of world records and his more successful Olympic achievements. Needless to say, the question can be looked at differently and it depends how you weight the different factors which might contribute to an assessment. One might compare the two runners as follows:

Outright speed – Coe Note (1)

Racing ability – Ovett Note (2)

Racing record – Coe Note (3)

Racing range – Ovett Note (4)

Note (1) It is a fact that Coe ran superior times. Over 800 metres, he was substantially quicker than Ovett – 1:41.73 versus 1:44.09. He also broke more world records than Ovett.

Note (2) Many consider Ovett to have had the superior racing ability. The most obvious evidence is that Ovett won Coe's specialist event, the 800 metres, in Moscow despite having a personal best which was some 1.5 seconds slower at the time. Coe himself considers Ovett's 1500 metres in the World Cup in Düsseldorf in 1977 to be the finest, most perfectly executed and dominant race he had ever seen.

Note (3) Although it can be argued that Ovett had superior racing ability, Coe's overall race record is certainly the better. Coe was back-to-back 1500 metres champion at the Moscow and Los Angeles Olympics and won 800 metres silver at both games as well. Interestingly, Coe never won Olympic gold at his favoured event and it was almost as if the various rounds of the 800 metres were a warm-up for the 1500 metres which came afterwards at both Olympics.

Note (4) Ovett's range of competitive ability was remarkable. He was, of course, Olympic 800 metres champion. He held world records at the 1500 metres and mile as well as over 2 miles. He was also the 1986 Commonwealth champion over 5000 metres and a cross country runner of considerable merit. Consider finally the barely credible statistic mentioned in Chapter 3: on 20th August 1977, just two weeks before his World Cup appearance over 1500 metres in Düsseldorf, Ovett ran 65 minutes for a half marathon in Dartford. It beggars belief that an athlete would even attempt a half marathon at that stage of preparation for a major 1500 metres race, never mind run the time he did. Ovett truly was a mercurial athlete at his peak.

In the final analysis, the true winner was the sport of athletics. Coe and Ovett brought sporting theatre of the most dramatic kind. They traded world records, scaled the Olympic peaks and, in Moscow, held the attention of the athletics world as none before them. They also spawned a remarkable crop of other British milers, including Steve Cram and Peter Elliott. In later years Coe and Ovett found that, despite their different backgrounds, they have plenty in common and have become friends. There never really was a "good guy" and a "bad guy": this was but a fictional creation of the press.

It is fair to say that no other athletics rivalry in this country has ever approached that of Coe and Ovett. They were super talents who were years ahead of their time and captured the imagination not just of diehard athletics fans but of the public at large. They were, and always shall be, towering icons of this great sport.

Ovett takes the 5000 metres title at the 1986 Commonwealth Games in Edinburgh

A trio of British supermilers at the Los Angeles Olympics

Coe takes the Olympic 1500 metres title in Los Angeles

Coe and Ovett in relaxed discussion at the Melbourne Commonwealth Games, 2006

Coe takes the Olympic 1500 metres title in Moscow

Ovett gives 110% as he races to victory in the 800 metres Olympic final

Appendices

Appendix I

The Moscow Results

The results of the 800 metres final on 26 July 1980 were as follows:

1. Steve Ovett (GBR) 1:45.4

2. Sebastian Coe (GBR) 1:45.9

3. Nikolay Kirov (URS) 1:46.0

4. Agberto Guimarães (BRA) 1:46.2

5. Andreas Busse (GDR) 1:46.9

6. Detlef Wagenknecht (GDR) 1:47.0

7. José Marajo (FRA) 1:47.3

8. Dave Warren (GBR) 1:49.3

The results of the 1500 metres final on 1 August 1980 were as follows:

1. Sebastian Coe (GBR) 3:38.4

2. Jürgen Straub (GDR) 3:38.8

3. Steve Ovett (GBR) 3:39.0

4. Andreas Busse (GDR) 3:40.2

5. Vittorio Fontanella (ITA) 3:40.4

6. Jozef Plachý (TCH) 3:40.7

7. José Marajo (FRA) 3:41.5

8. Steve Cram (GBR) 3:41.0

9. Dragan Zdravkovi? (YUG) 3:43.1

Appendix II
The Coe-Ovett Effect

One of the most fascinating aspects of the Coe-Ovett rivalry was the impact it had on middle distance running generally in the UK. Many will have heard of Steve Cram who was the most successful athlete to follow in the wake of Coe and Ovett. Cram went on to break the 1500 metres and mile records himself, taking many championship wins in the process. Olympic gold eluded him, though, and his best chance – at 1500 metres in the 1984 Los Angeles Olympics – was upset by Coe himself who, in a remarkable comeback from toxoplasmosis, took the title. Cram, however, remains the best middle distance athlete to come out of the UK since Coe and Ovett.

Another successful athlete was Peter Elliott, the gutsy runner from Yorkshire. Elliott too enjoyed considerable success at both 800 metres and 1500 metres and had some well-documented selection tussles with Coe. In almost any other country, Elliott would have been the number one middle distance athlete. But at the 1984 Olympics, the presence of Coe, Ovett and Cram meant that he didn't even get selected for the team.

Beyond Cram and Elliott, however, the UK had far more than its fair share of gifted world class athletes. Graeme Williamson, a talented Scot, was a teenage rival of Steve Cram but eventually fell away from the scene with injury. Then there was Steve Crabb, a superb miler with a best time of 3 minutes 52 seconds to his name and yet barely known to anyone other than fairly serious followers of the sport. Dave Moorcroft was another highly talented middle distance runner who enjoyed greater success over 5000 metres. It is less easy to say that Moorcroft emerged in the wake of Coe and Ovett – he was already enjoying major success by the late 1970s and early 1980s. But he was certainly touched by the success of Coe and Ovett and it is possible his move up to 5000 metres was influenced by them. The same can also be said of John Robson, the talented Scottish athlete. Tom McKean, another Scot who had much championship success over 800 metres, also deserves mention.

So the Coe-Ovett effect was considerable. If you look at the UK all time top 10 performances over 1500 metres, only three come from an era other than the 1970s and 1980s. It is a worthy testament to these great athletes and an interesting indictment of the funding programmes which exist today but which were absent in the Coe-Ovett era. In this historic year of 2012, we could rather do with their special talents.

About the Author

Hugh Shields has had a lifelong passionate interest in athletics. A serious runner himself, he won a Blue at Cambridge University and has competed for the Great Britain Masters team over 1500 metres and 3000 metres. Hugh is a member of Thames Hare and Hounds, Serpentine Running Club, Achilles AC and Scottish Veteran Harriers Club. Hugh lives in London with his wife and daughter.